Don't Be Averse To A Verse

by

Arthur Taylor

Contents

Foreword

If I was asked to dedicate this book to anyone it would be to my wife, Martha.

We felt we were meant for each other when we exchanged names: Martha and Arthur!

We were married sixty four years when she died.

Her sense of humour permeates this book, because I realise in retrospect she nudged my subconscious that influenced some of the poems.

I wrote some of these poems sixty years ago or more, so they reflect the morality of the times. The parochial humour of the Welsh Valley folk is engrained in some of my work along with the wonders of Creation, written at the risk of offending the Evolutionists.

Attitudes to marriage and morality have changed from the past, therefore I can only imagine the irritation this may cause some modernist thinkers. So please accept my thoughts simply as a history lesson.

~ A. Taylor

A Fou(w)l Ditty

A Chicken can't swim
It's a pity for him
Because if he went on the water
He'd immediately sink
And before he could blink
He'd realise he hadn't oughta

He's not like a Duck
Who has the good luck
Blessed with bones that aren't dense
Unlike the Chick
Whose bones are thick
Swimming wouldn't make sense

Between me and you
I wonder who
Made the Duck's bones hollow
Did it happen by luck
To the fortunate Duck?
I find that hard to swallow.

The Silver Artist

The magic of a moonlit night
Can easily pass us by
So we need to be aware of it
And watch with practised eye
Otherwise we would miss
The silent gilding of the land
Transforming almost everything
As if by some giant hand
Moonlight paint that needs no brush
Covers everything
Except where shadows black
Resist mass decorating
But suddenly, like an artist's sponge
There steals across the sky
A great black cloud blots out the moon
And there before your eye
The silver gilding melts away
Like frost before the sun
The Silver Artist's had his way
Now you see his work undone.

The Hat

Matthew and Blessing
Kept us all guessing
Wondering what they would wear
They turned up in style
And just for a while
They looked a dazzling pair
But the fact is Matt
Is returning the hat
Although it looked really super
But between you and me
The fact is, you see
He'd borrowed it from Tommy Cooper.

Home Cured

A pig went to the doctors
He was old and well matured
The doctor said: "You have to die
Before you can be cured."

"Do you mean," the old pig said
Feeling quite forsaken
"That the only thing I'm good for
Is smoked or home-cured bacon?"

"All I can say," the doctor said
Feeling quite irate
"You will end up very soon
As slices on a plate!"

"You can't be right."
The pig replied,
For he was big and burly
"Because my tail's sent me a message
That it's twirly." (too early)

Riding The Waves

Almost anyone can do it
Nearly everybody does
It's not a difficult thing to do
It's done by most of us.

You only have to say "I do"
And your partner agree
You leave the port of singleness
To sail the matrimonial sea.

But often, after setting sail
We find the sea gets rough
And the 'perfect partner' that you chose
Turns out to be quite rough.

It's always their fault, never ours
Whenever things go wrong,
Instead of being in harmony
Both sing a different song.

What a stupid way to live
Fighting every day
When God observes the way we live
I wonder what he would say.

Marriage was something God devised
It was He who made the rules
We can either apply them in our lives
Or ignore them and be fools.

If we are Christians, we've no choice
Because when we said "I do."
We didn't just promise our partner
We promised Jehovah too!

Oh To Be A Flea!

I wish I were a little flea
Living on a dog
I'd go for walkies every day
Keeping nice and snug
I'd bring up all my children
Protected by the cur
I'd teach them how to dodge its paws
When he scratched his fur
We'd even go on holidays
When summer comes to us
Maybe even find another dog
Or hop aboard a puss
But even if we found another dog
To whom to get attached
It wouldn't take us very long
To bring him up to scratch.

Mother Nature Gives Birth

As subtle as a brimming tear
Spilling gently down a careworn cheek,
Winter snows disappear
Flooding rivulet and creek.
From her warm heart Mother Earth releases
From protection into birth,
Young eager plants starting life anew,
Fulfilling every shade and hue.
As if to synchronise with sound,
This beauty which is all around,
The birds trill out their symphony
To herald nature's majesty.
With sound and sight we can now devour
The season's most bewitching hour,
Thus realise with appreciation,
The magnificence of God's creation.

The Caterpillar

As caterpillars go, I'm ugly I know
All green and hairy and fat
But what keeps me going is me knowing
I'll not always be like that

Some day ahead I'll retire to bed
I'll wake up, my green coat gone
And in place of those things
I'll have beautiful wings
All colours for the sun to shine on

I could never crawl fast,
That's a thing of the past
When I reach my bewitching hour
When I'll soar on my wings
And see beautiful things
As I fly from flower to flower

So if you think you're plain
Let me explain
That the same thing could happen to you
And in one golden hour
An invisible power
Will make you beautiful too.

Whether flying or crawling,
If you think you're appalling
Then that is how you will be
So don't try to hide what you are inside
Think beautiful thoughts like me.

If you think you're not nice
Take my advice
Which I give to you for free
Just think ahead, with me, as I said
When you'll be a butterfly with me.

Gentle Autumn

Gentle Autumn's changing ways
Are seen in sweet September
As she hangs onto Summer's tail
Trying to remember
The colours she has used before
Occupy her mind
She reaches through her memory file
For colours she needs to find
She experiments with shades of red,
Brown and burnished gold
And watches with satisfaction
Her colour scheme unfold
The magnitude of her work
Brings pleasure to our eyes
The approaching white of winter
She colourfully defies.

Evolution On The Beach

"I think I'd like to grow a leg."
Said the body on the beach.
"I've laid here two million years,
And there's places I'd like to reach."
"Don't hold your breath," the left hand said,
"Look what happened to me:
I waited here ten thousand years
Before they heard my plea."
"But what is a leg?" the right eye asked
"Will it bring improvement?"
"I should say," the body replied
"It will give me movement!"
"You'll need more than one," the eye replied
"If mobility you seek."
"What! Wait another million years?
You've got a flaming cheek!"

Mankind Tends To Mark The Spot

Mankind tends to mark the spot
Of someone claimed in death
Paying homage to lifeless mutes
With a sweetly scented wreath.
The recipients of his concern
On their journey to the dust
Cannot smell the flowers
Feel sorrowing or trust.
It's the mourning ones that feel the grief
With memories of the one
Who lies asleep beneath the earth
All their grieving done.
They feel no pain, no anguish,
No remorse, no jealousy
From the conscious cares of mortal man
Death brings immunity.

The Telephone Rang...

The telephone rang
It was Terry's voice
I knew right then
I had no choice
So I settled down
Feeling mean
And rubbed my ear
With vaseline
I knew what he wanted
I'd heard it before:
"I forgot points three and four.
Could you tell me again,
Brother please do.
I can add them then
To one and two.
Oh! Just one thing before you go,
Something else I'd like to know:
Was it three or one
Or two or four
That I rang you about before?
Because according to one
That was on my list,
It was three and two that I missed.
But it doesn't matter
It could have been four.
I'll ring you back
If there's any more!"

A Child's World

A world where everything is huge,
devoid of deception or subterfuge.
If an opinion is asked of a hat
they say they don't like it....
and that is that!
Pockets bulge with mixed collection
of string and washers, with sweet confection.
Half eaten apples and sea-shells meet
cheek by jowl with rabbit's feet.
On special days they are all disgorged,
spread out, counted and explored.
Then carefully collecting them from the floor,
back in the pockets they're stuffed once more.

A Party

Parties are cure-all
They have the magic touch
They even cause the those limping
To throw away their crutch
Many with a bad back
That seem limited by pain
Have been seen to do the rhumba
On the dance floor without strain.
Ailments seem to vanish
When party time begins
Faces filled with anguish
Are filled with vibrant grins
Appetites once lost seem to re-appear
When the magic word "party"
Is whispered in their ear
Walking sticks are thrown away
Zimmer frames left behind
As the magic of a party
Helps them to unwind
So until the New World
With it's permanent cure
They'll have to depend on parties
To heal them just once more.

Long Distance Loo – Part I

I asked to visit a friends toilet not realising it was about 25 yards down the garden – like a sentry box!

Nature called, I heard it strong,
We were dining with Steve in the land of song.
I said to him, "I'll have to go.
Show me your loo, and don't be slow."
He looked at me as if insane,
Saying, "Didn't you go before you came?"
I thought, "That's a funny expression to use,
He must have a complex about using his loo."
I looked at him with withering eyes,
With assurance I wasn't telling lies.
Steve said, "You'll have to wait a bit Butt,
While I get some sandwiches cut.
And while I'm about it, please make it plain
Would you rather go by bus or train?"
I desperately gasped, "All that I seek
Is to find your loo and have a leek."
He said, "Look here Arth, you poor old soul,
You'll just have to use some self-control.
If you don't believe me, ask my spouse,
Our loo is two miles from the house."
So with compass, road-map and candle bright,
I ventured off into the night,
But it took so long I'm afraid to state,
I found the flaming thing too late.

International Convenience – Part II

*The following year, we visited the same friends featured in
'The Long Distance Loo.' They'd had an indoor toilet
fitted. They were flushed with pride!*

It was mentioned in the U.N.
And in the House of Commons too.
Nearly brought the Lords to ruin,
Even caused the Queen to view!

People came from China saying
We would live to rue it.
Brezhnev from The Kremlin
Sent the K.G.B. to view it.

But especially in Treharris,
The people gazed in awe.
They had never seen a toilet
Inside a house before.

But Steve stood by it proudly,
Having stopped up all the leaks,
Gazing fondly at the monument
He'd been working on for weeks.

"Just look at that!" he said,
With a quiver in his voice.
"Oh! At last I can go now."
Said his wife (her name was Joyce)

Now every time they use it,
They think back with pride,
When they never had a toilet,
That they could use inside.

So next time you use their toilet,
Don't worry about the mess.
Just sit in admiration, and think of
Steve, flushed with success.

Winter

Emerging from her secret place
With ice-cold heart and frostbitten face
Rubbing frozen hands with anticipation
To her rival Autumn she pays attention
Breathing frosty breaths on this golden season
She puts to flight without reason
Spraying its end with heartless white
Chasing autumn warmth into the night
Now with her attention without distraction
Wintertime goes into action
Gripping plants with strangling, stiffening white
Carpet-laying frost at night
With no respect for plant or creature
Her merciless cold becomes a feature
Freezing ponds and stiffening grass
Crunching underfoot as people pass
Artistic though she may well be
Gilding fences, rooftops as well as tree
In a glistening coat so diamond bright
It even hurts the eyes at night
No colouring or change of hue
No shades of brown or green or blue
No! She'll persist in virgin white
Til Spring returns with colours bright
Undoing all that Winter's done
Banishing white with warmth of sun
As it burns off Winter's coat
Driving her to lands remote
In her cold heart she feels pain
Until she chases Autumn once again.

The March of Time

Tic toc insists the clock
Your impassive face I see
Your ever insistent moving hands
Are counting time for me.
Hey! That's my time you are ticking off,
I want to make it last
Your restless hands are never still,
Don't they ever rest?
Do you have to do time's will?
Are you its helpless slave?
Aren't you aware you're ticking off
The seconds to my grave?
Every day I look at you
Ticking off the time
Go easy with it can't you,
I tell you again, it's mine!
The trouble is dear time-piece
I know that you can count
But there's one thing you can't tell me:
How much time is in my account?

Dew

The dawn is enhanced by its lustrous presence
It carpets grass and trees
Refreshes flowers' faces
Answering Mother Nature's pleas
To wash the sleep from her children's eyes
Whether oak or elm or yew
The sun will rise and dry the eyes
Of cool refreshing dew.

<u>Seeing is Believing</u>

Oh! Woe is me! Woe is me!
I only believe what I can see.
In fact, as far as I'm concerned
There's no gas in coal that can be burned
As for that hoax called television
It really drives me to derision
How can a picture one-foot-nine
Squeeze through a wire that's so fine?
Why can the glow of a worm I see
When there is no battery?
What is it makes the wind blow so?
You don't see it come and you don't see it go!
You say it's God. I cannot agree,
If that God I cannot see
To me there's only one solution:
And that is the theory of evolution.

Spring

The cheeky face of spring appears
And smiles for all she's worth
Charming hidden seeds of many kinds
To come peeping through the earth.
Their heads appear in coloured hats
Of many shades and hues
Insects fly from flower to flower
Spreading the good news.
"She's here!" they cry. "She's here!" they cry
"Come on out! Don't hide!
Winter's gone Spring has come
the sun is on her side."
The flowers respond, shy at first
Then they hear the insects cry
But soon they lose their timidity
And raise their heads up high.

The Operation

To approach the Irilim
We entered from the back
Administering an epidural
Then took up the slack
We exposed the Omniphlatablotus
Which looked healthy and benign
The Spudibloctive nerve below
Was also looking fine
The Caratotive valve revealed
Acidotic burns
Which affected its efficiency
Causing some concern
A Parsatonic spasm
In the Clackerbox
Seemed to cause the patient
Aphrodilic shock
So we tightened the Ochrilium
And released the Puttaflochs
Allowing the Achrodonic fluids
To arrest the universal shock
At the conclusion of the treatment
We conferred and made it known
That the patient would have been better off
If we had left well alone!

Disaster's Path

Man doubted God and went his way,
thus laid foundations for decay
Of the whole world of humankind
who went ahead… with God behind
God didn't need to keep them in sight
He just followed the wreckage of their plight
Disease and war, corruption, crime
confronted God all the time.
As he observed the path man chose
to God the evidence arose
To testify without any doubt
that time for man was running out.
Instead of saying "I told you so."
this loving God let all men know
that he was prepared to rescue them,
And he would be their God again.
Although he gave his only son
to rescue man from what man had done,
Not many cast aside their doubt
and accepted that this was God's way out
of a wicked system trapping man
that bore testimony to the Devil's plan
Despite evidence, mountain high
that reasonable ones cannot deny
The vast majority of man
will deny the Devil's plan
And all because when he set out
man allowed Satan to cast doubt
Soon before the final curtain
God will establish (and this is certain)
a New System for those who love
and never doubt their God above.

Class of '84

I saw the class of '84
That first day they came through the door,
At first sight they looked forlorn,
As if blown in by a passing storm.
That first day I'll never forget,
Their appetites we tried to whet
As they sat there missing mam,
And all that lovely bread and jam.
But as the days went fleeting by,
Although we really had a try
To satisfy their appetites,
I'm afraid we lost the fight.
They shovelled food into their faces,
Putting their stomachs through their paces,
They ate apples, trifles, cakes at will,
Then started on the daffodils.
They may have arrived with inhibitions,
But in just two weeks there were transitions.
From a weedy, sickly-looking lot
Who are going home with an extra pot.
It did us good to see them eat,
Filling hollow legs and hollow feet.
Just think, I knew them when they were lissom!
But I must admit, I won't arf miss 'em.

Love Birds

"I notice," said the Cockatoo
To his friend the Parakeet
"All those people going to church
Halfway down our street.
I wonder what they do there?"
He asked the pagan Pigeon.
"Oh, I know," the Pigeon said
"It's to practice their religion!"
"They've been practicing a long time."
Quietly cooed the Dove
"I've been helping them," the Seagull cried
"By dropping messages of love."
"What colour's love?" the Parakeet asked
"Would I recognise it by sight?"
"Of course you would," the Seagull said
"It's all soft and wet and white."
"Does that mean," said the Cockatoo
"What we see from above
Aren't statues covered in Pigeon poo,
But are encrusted in our love?"
"I don't think people appreciate
That we show them care
Dropping messages of love
As we fly through the air."
"I'm sure they don't," a voice cried out
Belonging to the Sparrow,
"They came around the other day
And removed it in a barrow."
"Folks are not aware, I know
That every time I spot them
That it is a message of love
From the heart of my bottom."
They all agreed, except the Dove
With a collective frown
That all of them in future
Would be flying upside down.

Gone With The Wind

With innocent looks upon their face,
They really are a dire disgrace
Those cows with large unblinking eyes
Standing there you would surmise
That they were harmless chewers of cud,
Don't let their 'innocence' fool you bud.
As they stand there chewing grass
They are manufacturing methane gas
Which they release so silently,
Spelling doom for you and me
It's them that's caused the ozone gap
With the occasional thunderclap!
If you're wondering how they do,
They use the opposite end from which they moo,
So just remember they ain't so dumb
They can do more damage with their bum
Than Hitler did in World War Two.
So that's why I'm warning you:
When next you see a bovine beast,
If the wind is west
YOU GO EAST!

A Lifetime

I fell asleep upon my bed
And dreamt about the life I'd led
It was as if my brain cells had elected
To have my memories resurrected
Memories I thought were dead
Went racing through my sleeping head
My first entry into school, the smell of chalk
The teacher's stool, lead pencils, ink wells
Pens with nibs, teacher scolding as I crib
My father, giant with prickly skin
That reddened my face as I cuddled him
The down-like softness of my mother's breast
Where I lay my head when seeking rest
I saw in picture my first kiss
Pursing my lips in expectant bliss
The grey day when my mother died
My shrunken father as he cried
The smell of flowers, people in black
A consoling ride on my uncle's back
Silent house like a quiet grave
My father trying to be brave
Holding me tighter than ever before
Our tears blending on the floor
My first love, our troth plighted
Swearing forever to remain united

Ere a week had gone, love struck once more
This time with the boy next door
My face reddened and bright with rouge
His plastered hair and boots so huge
I remembered clearly my first dance
The dress I wore, then real romance
The wedding, guests, presents many
My mean auntie who hadn't given any
The awkwardness of that first night
When neither would put on the light
Our first child – my size amazing
As I see my reflection while window-gazing
My father, not a giant now
With wrinkled hands and wrinkled brow
His faded eyes alight with joy
A grandson! Yes, it was a boy
In my unconscious state I found
As my memories unwound
That really life is very fleeting
And soon our earthly end we're meeting.
The Bible's words of James are searing
Like a mist ... then disappearing
When my life began it looked so endless
In retrospect it's really much less.

The Blind Spot

It's not so easy you'll agree
To see yourself as you see me
In my eyes I have no faults
Yet myself I don't exalt
Whereas you are rarely right
And physically you are a sight
Not like me: handsome tall
I have no blemishes at all
And anything I say or do
Is bound to be in advance of you
When it comes to an argument
Your opinion's not worth a cent
The trouble is I know it all
I've never been wrong as I recall
Every decision I have made
Has put all others in the shade
So it's no good trying to better me
I'm as perfect as can be
Being strong, intelligent, refined
Generous, clever, modest, kind
You inferiors agree with me
And acknowledge my superiority
But don't look too close or you will find
The truth is, really I am blind
By that I don't mean I can't see
I just can't find a fault in me.

Looking Back

In the twilight of the years as you sit
  holding hands all toothless
You reflect upon your married life,
  feeling rather useless.
You remember well the happy day,
  you thought you'd never rue it
But now as you look back you think,
  "Whatever made me do it!"
You think of all those carefree days,
  dining out and roller-skating
When neither of you minded
  if the other kept you waiting
But now it's "Are you ready, I'm not waiting!"
  that's the shout
Or, "Aren't we going out again!
  You never take me out!"
You each recall what it was
  that was the main attraction
She was Wonder Woman
  and he was Man of Action
Now you each reflect with watering eyes
  On the person that you wed
And think whatever it was the other had
  It's now stagnant, if not dead.
But all is not for nothing,
  as you think back down the years
You remember well the happiness,
  as well as all the tears
And suddenly it dawns on you,
  and both are stirred to say,
"My dear I wouldn't have wanted it any other way."

The Pyramids of Wales

Wales! The land of pyramids grey
Put there by man and there to stay
Born from man's digging deep
Rejected as useless, they wouldn't keep.
Therefore cast upon this growing mound
Coming deep, deep from underground
To form a man-made mountain of useless soil
Shaping giant symbols from man's toil
Like massive sentinels waiting to grow
Patiently waiting supplies from below
That results from the work of coal-blacked slaves
Who live a mole-like existence in their coal-black caves
The black stuff that these men sought
Is clothed with the slag which they abort
They send it up into the light of day
To add to the growth of mountains grey
Though rejected as useless and counts for nought
It survives the coal that man sought
Feeding our fires, the coal didn't survive
Yet the useless slag remains alive.

My Special Tree

Not many things in our lives
Prove to be reliable
But the durability of a tree
Is really undeniable.
When I visit my favourite tree
I need never care
I know without a shadow of doubt
That it will definitely still be there
It has stood there since I don't know when
Swaying in the breeze
Nodding to the passer's by
With its head of leaves
When I sit beneath its boughs
Admiring its beauty
It shelters me from the rain
As if it were its duty
Winter will soon be on its way
When we can compare
This proud trees appearance
Without Mother Nature's hair
Spring will soon be here though
I can hardly wait til then
To see Mother Nature help my tree
To grow its hair again.

Dai's Mystery Trip

Hello Dai, how are you?
Is that suit you've got brand new?
And those shiny shoes upon your feet,
Did you buy them in St. Mary Street?
And what is the idea, Dai,
A clean white shirt with collar and tie?
Only once before did I see you the same
'Twas your granny's funeral to blame
But I haven't heard that anyone's died
Or that you're fixed up with a bride,
So for the life of me I can't think why
You're all dressed up in a collar and tie.
You don't dress like that for the Band of Hope
And you were never very fond of soap,
So you can't blame me if I look stupid,
Don't tell me… you've been shot by Cupid!
Come on Dai, tell me who
Has inspired this change in you,
Oh! 'It's not a girl,' you say,
You're going to Cardiff to see Wales play.

Depression

Depression is an ugly thing
that claims its victims by subtle means,
It beclouds our minds when we are low
misting all our treasured dreams.
It approaches not from one direction
but captures us in many ways
Causing gloom and dark to settle,
blocking out our hope's bright rays.
At such times our minds turn inwards,
seeking to feed on bitter thoughts.
Ignoring comfort that is proffered,
despondency sails into port.
If we allow this ship of gloom
to anchor firm within our hearts,
The port may close and we'd be left
without access to better parts.
At such times we need the spirit
of a warm enlightening God
Help count our blessings, lift our heads up
and give our selfish hearts a prod.
We will then find as we compare
ourselves with others' tragic plight
Depressing dark despair will lift,
self-centred thoughts will take to flight.
A marvellous way to heal depression
is to look outside ourselves,
Thus forgetting all our worries
as in the Word of God we delve.
It's there we find uplifting thoughts
Inspired by the Holy One,
Dispelling all morbidity,
farewell to gloom and welcome sun.

Reverse Advancement

In a speed-increasing world
Where jet-planes scream and 'copters whirl
Where high-speed trains roar down the track,
Faster than ever, there and back
Where turbo cars are all the fashion,
And foreign motorbikes the passion
In a world where speeds are super plus
We're still waiting for the bus!

Equality

Where one's born it matters not
It neither matters what one's got
It's what we are that really counts
And to what our attributes amount
Our love, our kindness and integrity
Our sense of justice, our generosity
Geography does not determine
The type of person to which we turn in
It's the qualities we cultivate
That shape our destiny – not fate.

Oh! That I Could Sleep!

They brought me to this restful place
Equipped with beds galore
They told me that I wasn't well
My health was really poor
"You need to rest." The doctor said
As he gazed with a pitiful face
"You need a few days in a cosy bed."
So they sent me to this place.
The beds were clean, sheets shiny white
And comfortable as well
"Just the job," I gladly thought
But wait! There's more to tell
Slumber had all but claimed me
When an icy hand descended
"Can I have a sample of your blood?"
My dream of peace had ended
At fairly frequent intervals
A nurse in pristine white
Sought my cooperation
Throughout the day and night
Bladder checks and temperatures
Shaves and test reflexes
They came at me from all sides
They were made up of both sexes
But never mind, they're a lovely lot
And I know they do their best
But I look forward to going home
So I can have some rest!

Imagination

In the soft descending gloom
I peered intently across my room
It held for me fond memories
Accumulated by degrees
So what was it that I could see
That eluded tantalisingly?
You my love had long since gone
Yet your presence lingered on
It pervaded, clung to everything
You needed no remembering
You were there! Your presence strong
In the room where you belong
Complete in your identity
Still living in my memory
Ah! Now 'tis clear what I see
In misty, veiled imagery
It's your face distilled from secret yearning
Manifesting what I'm discerning
You've returned my love
But there's no elation
It's only in my imagination.

A Type of Letter

I lot a letter the other day
It proved to be an **S**
Now when I write a letter
I'm really in a me
Although I hout and holler
And wear and tamp my feet
I till can't find that letter
I dropped in the treet
o until I find it
All I can ugget
I'll ign my letter
And end you all the bet.

A Sad Cloud's Lesson

It hung there, suspended in the sky
an enormous, majestic cloud
It regally, yet sedately, drifted by
impressively white and proud.

Propelled invisibly, it sailed along
traversing silently in flight
Giving the impression it was strong,
and independent satellite.

But then the cloud began to cry
its tears descending to the earth
Distributing its liquid sadness
not realising its true worth.

As eager foliage far below
Stretched their heads to meet the tears
Their leaves were washed, thirsts were quenched
A sad cloud had brought them cheer.

Why can't we be like that cloud
so that even in our sadness
We'll contrive to do some useful acts
contributing to other's gladness.

The Lessons Of Old Age

I am learning to live with old age
Which is like being confined to a cage
The bars that affect my daily life
Causing frustration and unknown strife
Are not made of wood, iron or steel
But limit my life and make me feel
That my limbs don't respond to the things I know
Things I did not so long ago
Age reminds when I bend or climb stairs
It's interfering with my physical affairs
If I sit down I can't rise
And cataracts blur my eyes
I leave the room with my mind set
But when I get where I am, I forget
What was it I wanted I couldn't remember
I don't even know if it's May or September
Although old age brings it's sorrow
I hope that I'm alive tomorrow!

OH! Susannah!

Susannah's nose was glowing
You could see her in the dark
Curtis was amazed at this luminary lark
"How do you do that?"
Said Curtis all excited.
"I could hire you as floodlights
To Manchester United."
"Cor!" said Ellis with a grin
"That's quite a conk you've got
It looks more like a 100 than a 40 watt."
"Yes," said Liam, still in shock
"You really look a sight
But you will come in handy
If we blow a fuse tonight."
"Can't you see I'm radioactive,"
Cried Susannah with elation.
"If I have any more from you
I will give you radiation."
The three lads got together
And pooled their cash with glee
And paid for Susannah
To have a Hooterectomy!

Bed Bound

If you're feeling poorly
And sorry for yourself
Think of us while laying there
Suffering good health!
We hope you'll soon be better
And remember what we've said
And give some healthy people
A chance to lay in bed!
We're sorry you're on the sick
And feeling kind of queer,
But we trust you will be better soon
And give us cause to cheer!

An Ode to Christine

She's well known for her 'get well' cards
She sends to one and all,
You'll get one even if you're fit,
Just in case you fall.
The odes of love she fills them with
Often make you swoon,
The last card I received from her
Was entitled, 'Get Sick Soon.'
When she was young and single
She would sit up most the night
Racking her brains for poems
To cheer a sick one's plight.
But now that she is married
She has other things to do
Such as sending cards to chimney sweeps
She thinks have caught the flu.
So if you're feeling poorly
And a card comes to your home
It's a million to one she sent it
Containing her latest poem.

The Too Good to Hurry Curry!

I've eaten food in China
Tibet and Timbuktu
But I've never eaten anything
like mother's curry, vindaloo
She's an amazing cook is mother
her abilities never cease
She can do for edible food
what Hitler did for peace
Her potatoes, peas and fishcakes
are a true gourmet delight
They keep you going through the day...
and halfway through the night
So whatever's on the menu
eat and have no fear
The resurrection's certain
and the paradise is near!

Changing Times

Gone are the days of long ago
When you spoke to people you didn't know
When "After you" was a common expression
When one rarely heard, "I've got depression!"
When shop assistants were polite
and you were not afraid to walk at night
When there was no such thing as a mobile 'phone
and dirty language you would not condone
When you knew if two people 'tied the knot'
one was female and the other not!
When women's clothes were dignified
and not designed for nothing to hide
When home was viewed with appreciation
and not just as a filling station.
When as soon as you came through the door
you'd shout, "Hello Mum!" for you were sure
That she'd reply, because you always knew
she would be there to welcome you.

Tree-mend-us

When I visit my special tree
It's like as if it talks to me
Its hair of leaves sways in the breeze
I am sure it's me it's trying to please
I often hear my lovely tree
Whispering its love for me
It lifts my spirits to banish despair
My favourite tree is always there
It never deserts me or goes away
It's a symbol of true love
It's there to stay!

Can You Imagine?

Can you imagine God's New World
Where an endless future will be unfurled?
Can you imagine a world without pain
Where there'll be no doctors to call again?
Can you imagine when arising
Feeling great? That will be surprising!
Can you imagine no pollution
And not a mention of evolution?
Can you imagine that you are there
Living a life beyond compare?
Can you imagine you will never die
Or experience anything to cause a sigh?
Can you imagine every minute
Being filled with pleasure and you in it?
Can you imagine the return to life
Of your Mother, Father, child or wife?
Can you imagine a world with me
Who you'll have to put up with permanently?
But you cannot imagine however you try
How great it will be for you and I!

Stay Tuned

It cannot be seen, cannot be touched
Yet it can please one very much
It can make one laugh or make one cry
It can soothe, elate, or pacify
Although invisible it may be
It's effect one oft can see
Produced by one or two or more
Can be loud or soft uncertain sure,
Peaceful, stirring, smooth or lilting
Revives the spirit when they're wilting
It conjures pictures in the mind
Of golden days left far behind
By this God-given legacy
We're blessed by music you and me.

The Beanfeast

An explosion occurred the other day
We thought it was the IRA
When we went to investigate
We thought we had arrived too late
The roof was gone, the windows smashed:
The house next door was now detached
The scene was one of total ruin
The police asked Stan, "What were you doing?"
Stan stood there, his face all red,
He said, "I'd only just got into bed!
I'd had this feeling in my Jeans,
I shouldn't have ate so many beans.
You see for them I have a passion
Try as I may I cannot ration
And that's what happened, I'm afraid to say,
I'd been eating Beans all day!
Seventeen tins one after another,
That's the truth I tell you brother,
I thought, I'll have one for the road,
'Twas then I started to explode,
So please don't blame the IRA
For the damage you see here today
And warn the people about this scene,
And of the awesome power of beans.
Warn them all that every can
Can transform you into Superman.
That's why I eat them cooked or fried
For the power they give me inside
But there's one thing I am sad about,
My wife decided to kick me out.
She packed my bags and wished me well,
Because she couldn't stand the smell.
So really, that's my greatest moan,
I always end up on my own!!!"

Faith With Action

The everyday wishing that accompanies all
  In their secret quest for fulfillment
Rarely materialises for anyone who depends
  On wishes alone
Greatness maybe thrust on some when personal
  Endeavour is absent
But for the vast majority attainments are achieved
  Where hearts condone
The thoughts distilled from rich and ambitious
  Imagination
This being the first faltering step in
  A march of hope
But as with all things, little is achieved
  Minus imagination
Otherwise, we may be condemned with those
  Who blindly grope
With eyes of ambition stigmatised and
  Invariably closed
They unseeingly wish, having no regard
  For necessary action
So when opportunities, though sylph-like knock
  They are indisposed
Consequently, there is for them no
  Interaction
Between their ability to effortlessly concoct
  Magnificent plans
And the energy it takes to bring them
  To satisfaction
The seeds of desire lack the soil to make
  A dreamer a successful man.

The Princess Turns the Tables

Have you heard of the tale of Dave Riddel
who found himself by a wishing well
"What can I wish for?" pondered Dave
Then he had a great brainwave!
"I know what I'll do, I'll wish for a mate,
before it gets too flaming late."
He closed his eyes and expressed his wish,
"If it's not too late, make her a dish."
When he opened his eyes what do you think?
there was this vision dressed in mink!
"Oh! I hope you've arrived to say I will,
What's your name?" She said, "Phyl."
"You are what I've waited for,
I will love you forevermore!"
"Let's seal our meeting with a kiss
And enter into a life of bliss."
He pursed his lips his eyes were closed.
Phyl stood on her tippy toes.
He felt her kiss and thought, 'How sweet.'
It curled his toes on both his feet!
But he wasn't such a lucky dog
Cos when Phyl looked she saw a Frog
"Is that you Dave?" she cried, all choked
But all she got was a constant croak!

Secret Ambitions

Do you dream you are someone else
And picture in your mind
Another person of great renown
Strong, and good and kind?
Whereas in reality you are just like me,
An ordinary person without notoriety
We live our mundane, sober lives
Lacking their extremes
Hence we ordinary folk
Resort to secret dreams.

Good Times Ahead!

Silent as it seems to be
It's tragic effects are there to see
Empty streets that once were thriving
No visitors or friends arriving
I wait alone and wonder when
We'll touch physically again
No tender touch or fraternising
But really that is not surprising
We've been warned 'take no chance'
And help stop this virus advance
But we're not surprised we're unaffected
We've been scripturally directed
Long ago the Bible said
Things would happen that we would dread
This cloud of evil has a silver lining
Through which hope is clearly shining
All the signs of this devastation
Simply heralds our salvation
Very soon there'll be no fear
Hallelujah! The Kingdom's here!

True Reflections

You look at me a thousand times
   and see me every day
Although I've served you well and true,
   there's not a word you say
I tell you when you're looking smart
   or adjustments to be made
I always tell the truth to you,
   of that I'm not afraid.
If it wasn't for me you would never know
   the truth about your face
But with just a glance I tell you
   if everything's in place
In privacy, you peer at me
   as you would with no one else
Pulling funny faces
   and admiring yourself
Next time you need to look my way
   on my services to call
In case you have forgotten,
   I'm your mirror on the wall!

Hope Shines Through

Feeling sad, despondent, low
My mind had no place to go
Up blind alleys my thoughts sped
I was a prisoner in my own head
I could find no way out
of this darkened track of doubt
Oh! How I longed to see the light
that would release me from this plight.
It came one day when a dear friend
helped my damaged thoughts to mend
All he did was to be kind
and that shone light into my mind
that helped to banish crippling doubt
and let dark despondency seep out
It helped me then to realise
I'd misjudged myself in my own eyes
That someone saw in me some good
I'm so thankful for the brotherhood.

Happy Blues

I had Bluebells in my garden
Tall and aromatic
I picked some for my friends
They really were ecstatic
They scented the air in their room
Making breathing a delight
The glistening blue of the bells
Proved a splendid sight
"Thank you," said these friends of mine
"We appreciate them you know."
"Don't thank me," I replied
"It was Jehovah who made them grow."

Unseen Miracle

A little girl arrived for Kay
Her happiness we detected,
The little mite was welcome,
Though totally unexpected.
The moral to this story is,
Don't take things for granted,
Because seeds can only grow
Whenever they are planted!

She Is Unforgettable

Martha, I cannot forget you
You are deep within my heart
Why? Oh why my dearest love
Did we ever have to part?
Life without you can never be the same
My heart still leaps within me
At the mention of your name
We still meet in my dreams
But it only brings despair
When I awake to consciousness
I find that you're not there!

Ebtide!

Jim was from East Kilbride
He was born with some seashells inside
He married Jean
But the trouble has been
He keeps going out with the tide!

Hi Jean

There was a lady named Jean
Who fell into her washing machine
She told Jim with a grin
She'd just gone for a spin
But was glad to be back nice and clean!

Bad Spellars Ov The Whirled - Untie!

I have a spelling checker
It came with my PC
It plane lee marks four my revue
Miss steaks aye can knot sea

Remember This?

I am trying to remember
something I'd forgot
I wasn't sure
if I had forgotten it or not.
From the filing system in my brain
I used the re-call section
But all I got every time:
"Engaged! Is in rejection."
I wondered what was wrong with me
and sat there in dismay.
Why was it I could remember
what I wanted to forget that day?
Yet what I wanted to recall
the answers I could not find
what on earth is happening
to this thing I call a mind!

Evil-ution

As I was walking down the street
On the end of my legs I found my feet
All I could do was stand and stare
And wonder who had put them there
I asked my Priest, who said to me
"They've evolved, it's plain to see,
And in a million years or so,
You'll develop threads upon your toes."
Just think how beneficial that would be
Because if I bought shoes too small for me
I wouldn't complain or suffer loss
I'd remove my socks and screw my toes off!

As It Used To Be

Echoes of the distant past
came drifting through the mist
Reminding me of many things
some of which I'd missed
The yesterdays of long ago
seem so different now
as changes that have taken place
seem not so good somehow.
Marriage was a standard thing
that one looked forward to
Sincere in our sacred vows
to the one we gave them to
It wasn't trial and error then
or just to taste forbidden fruit
One made sure that the one we wed
would permanently suit!

Rescued From The Dust

Some time ago I went to sleep
it seemed just like a minute.
I woke up in the New World.
and thought, "Can it be I'm in it?"
I soon realised this is no dream
my pains had disappeared
The troubled thoughts I used to have
had gone with all my fears

My eyes adjusted to the scene
and I could smell the flowers
How long had I been sleeping?
It surely can't be hours!
Then I heard a familiar voice
saying, "Welcome home my Sweet,
I've been anxiously waiting for you and I to meet."
It was my darling husband
we kissed so tenderly
'Twas as if I'd left him yesterday
as he held on to me!

We both wept together
and I realised the years
had been greater than I thought
so much older were my dears
Whilst I had been asleep and
impervious to pain
I am now restored to life
and my family again

Now life is void of sickness
no worries or remorse
Death is done away with
and so has sin of course.
Every day I wake up
remembering what God had said
If I remained faithful
eternity lies ahead.
Joy fills my heart, me knowing
that Jehovah remembered me
Rescuing me from the dust
to life eternally!

The Fundamentalist

May I strike a blow for the fundamentalist!!

Born and raised in a television-less world of starting handles, manual tin openers, corner shops, steam locomotives and ink pens. I find myself surrounded by a system, devised and developed by a type of man that progressively scorns the mutts of my generation for our fundamental beliefs; thus I have been forced to make an assessment with the distinct advantage of knowing the world that the present generation of so-called intellectuals have used as a springboard from which to launch themselves into a mental and moral acrobatic dive from which it hasn't yet descended.

I ponder on the pre-school days when the pre-occupation of my mother was with a carpet-less, vacuum cleaner-less, washing machine-less, fridge-less, love-filled home.

A slap-threatened misdemeanour resulted in the threatened slap, there were no empty promises!!

Home was certainty where mother was, and father came home to after a hard days work.

Today's cosseted child is pitied by me as I make the comparison. In a T.V. dominated infancy, expediency seems the factor, generally speaking. Anything for peace!!

The wife that isn't working is invariably bored as the automatic washing machine in its robot-like functions, sloshes, washes, dries and airs fabrics that never need the attention of an iron.

The carpeted, chip-boarded, plastic, centrally heated filling stations called 'home' are a far cry from the happy, safe surroundings of my pre-school days, void though it may have been of today's electronic wizardry.

The very firmness of my parental discipline was like a warm blanket (non-electric) of safety and love. Their very authority was a haven to return to as I entered the world of schools and teachers, even in my moments of faltering timidity, at the back of my mind was the fact that Mum and Dad were always there.

The biological process hasn't changed for producing children – it's what we do with them once we've got them that's altered..... and keeps altering.

Self expression is essential! Don't punish, you may stunt a genius! The gospel of Spock guided the thinking of millions. I wonder how his disciples feel now that their god has repudiated his own doctrine?

Discipline in school was as much of an education as education; it cultivated loyalty rather than division, respect rather than resentment.

It's only in later life that I realised the genuine respect and affection that our headmasters and teachers accrued for themselves. Even the most authoritarian of them were never viewed as ogres, and in my case I relished the idea of the second generation going through their hands.

My fundamentalism extends even further, Yes, I believe in creation.

I believe the Bible is God's written word.

It is not religion, it's logic when a book recorded by about forty writers acting as God's secretaries, written over a period of one thousand six hundred years, describes the sequence of world powers before they took place. A book that foretells the precarious conditions that would exist in today's society, and even the attitudes of people in general; read at your leisure 2 Timothy 3 and the first five verses.

Now I can almost hear the modern theorists with their carbon clocks and evolutionary tables, laughing in derision. There's no room for the fundamentalist in their scientific society. Their trouble is they conveniently allot millions or billions of years to fashion their theories. How handy to be so liberal with a commodity that they never owned or controlled – Time!

Yet, when I look at the fundamental law of Genesis, they still hold true, everything is still producing after its own kind, although there may be variations within those kinds.

The shape of the earth described in Isaiah 40 verse 22: "There is one dwelling above the circle of the earth....." (the Hebrew word for circle is also translated sphere or orb) testifies to the knowledge of the writer, whereas, it's only three hundred-odd years ago that modern man discovered that fact.

Where did Isaiah's knowledge come from? Certainly not by scientific instruments, or from Scientists. It could only have come from the God of the Bible, dictating by Holy Spirit, His own knowledge to the benefit of mankind.

I have a daily benefit from the unchanging stability of the Bible in a constantly changing world; and I'm not so dumb! If the Bible is right, I'm on a winner! If it were wrong? I haven't lost a thing!!

A Computer Romance

'Twas twentyeight years ago today
David wed his Joan
Their happiness is evident
By all whom they are known
But if you trace their history
There are some surprises
The first thing David asked his Joan
Concerned academic prizes!
"Have you got a GCE? Or a pass in science?"
Which elicited from Joan
A firm look of defiance.
"You can take me as I am!" she cried
"Or go to the Devil.
I haven't got a science degree,
But I've got a Spirit Level!"
"That'll do for me," said Dave.
"I'll act as your tutor,
The first thing that you've got to learn
Is to work on my computer."
So Joan worked hard, applied herself
To learn 'computer speak'
As she discussed with David
The programmes for the week.

As the weeks and months went by
It became apparent
Cautious David found in Joan
A lady of real talent.
"Oh! Marry me!" David cried
"Before it is too late,
Even my computer's
Getting in a state."
"Oh alright," said Joan
With a nonchalant air,
"I suppose it would be cheaper
If we pooled all our Software."
So here they are together
Still making a great team
But with a dual-controlled computer,
Still their greatest dream!

A Brain for Sale
(hardly used!)

I went to the doctor the other day
I keep forgetting things a lot
He asked, "Why have you come to see me?"
I said, "I don't know. I forgot."

I went to the doctor the other day
Concerned with my memory lapses.
"I know what's wrong," the doctor said
"It's the gapses between your synapses."

Hair Apparent

I went to the Barber the other day
for him to cut my hair
"Good morning sir," he smiled at me,
"Please sit in the chair."
"Before we start," the Barber said,
"There is something I should say.
I'll have to charge you extra
for a follicle survey."
"What do you mean?" I replied
"I don't think that's fair!"
"You don't understand," the Barber cried,
"But it's a job to find your hair!"
He set about his task with a magnifying glass
Then suddenly he cried,
"I'm sorry to have to tell you
you are follically deprived!
But nevertheless I've found four hairs
which presents me with a riddle.
Do you want them parted on the left?
Or straight down the middle?"
As a gesture of goodwill
he gave me a toothless comb
Which was especially designed
for my hairless dome!

Goodbye El Salvador!

Adios El Salvador,
We may not see you any more,
But our memories will never fade
Of this marvellous visit we have made.
Mountains tall, volcanoes high
That seem to reach up to the sky,
Hills of green, skies of blue,
Vegetables and fruits we never knew.
Pot-holed roads and drivers mad
Gave us thrills we'd never had.
Markets with a thousand smells,
Everyone with things to sell.
Lovely bays and boisterous seas,
Giant Palms and coconut trees.
Water shortage, power cuts,
Poor people living in patched-up huts.
Battered lorries belching smoke
Causing everyone to choke.
This lovely jewel in the sun,
Reminds us of what God has done.
Giving man this lovely place
And sees him treat it with disgrace.

Advice
(From one who knows)

Incredible as it may seem
John has realised his dream
I said to John, "Please do beware,
It could turn out a real nightmare."

Why do you think she chose today?
Not just the 13th but also Friday!
I think your luck is in decline
You've just married Miss Frankenstein!

But now that she has landed you
Don't be surprised at what she'll do
But things won't get really bad
As long as you hide your Credit Card.

And never mind what she's said
You'll never get her out of bed.
She works regularly, Yes sir!
....One day every other year!

She knows although she is nice looking
You're going to suffer from her cooking
But when you eat her meals don't be afraid
Just make sure you learn First Aid!

When she said to you, "I will."
Did you know she's known as 'Spare-part Lil'
So you should know before you start,
She has an account with Unipart!

Don't get me wrong, I'm not beefing
I kissed her once without her teeth in.
And saw hanging from the chair
A wig I thought was her real hair.

So check your accounts John, I beg
'Cos when she recently bought a leg
She complained to her Mother
That it wasn't bowed to match her other.

Every night you'll be bereft
When you see what you've got left
You really will be in despair,
Most of her will be on the chair!

Now the truth is I envy you,
I really don't know what I'll do
When I go to the Kingdom Hall
And she won't be there at all.

We love her really, and wish her well,
And hope from this that you can tell
That we want you both to be
Just as happy as Martha and me.

Laughter

Laughter is a medicine
  that banishes the gloom
It brightens up the shadows
  when it fills a room.
Laughter is contagious
  and if you are infected
You'll no doubt, pass it on,
  but still remain affected.
If you laugh with others,
  especially at yourself
It eliminates your pride
  and contributes to your health.
It's a sound that's very special,
  does not consist of words
And yet it's understood
  wherever it is heard.
Sometimes we suppress,
  thinking it's undignified
But would we consider it an indignity
  if we broke down and cried?
No! You see it's an emotion
  that's as natural as can be
So let your laughter fill the air
  and disperse misery.
Different things make people laugh,
  we're not all the same
Some do it for a living
  acquiring great fame.

But if we make others laugh
  simply for the fun
We may never be a famous nut,
  but we'll be loved by everyone.
There are different types of laughter,
  and we should all beware
So that the type that we indulge in
  should be kind and sweet and fair.
To laugh at others downfalls
  is not the healthy kind
If others laughed at us that way
  we should lose our peace of mind.
So even in our laughter
  we can evidence our love
Reflecting qualities of a happy God
  that rules us from above.
So let's all laugh with kindness,
  encouraging one and all
To be a blessing to each other
  so laughter lifts us when we fall.

She Is Beautiful

I've known her from her early youth
Long before we knew the Truth
Slender, beautiful and sunny
Alert, alive and very funny
Her smile was wide
Her eyes large brown
Her face had never worn a frown
She's changed since then
Time's had it's way
Makes its demands every day
Swollen knees and arthritic hands
Pain still making its demands
Her youthful body once so slender
Submits to age in complete surrender
Shoulders sag and with shuffling gait
"I'm sorry dear, you'll have to wait."
Is her plea as she tries
To quicken her pace
But age denies!
In all these years that we've been wed
Seeing the life that she has led
Serving her God and family
Always as busy as she could be
She's journeyed from youth through her life
Being mother, grandmother and wife
Taking everything in her stride
The bread of laziness she could not abide
She's reached a point where age has won
And pain is blotting out the sun
But age's victory is only fleeting
Soon the New World we'll be greeting
Because of her loyalty to God's Truth
She'll be returned to eternal youth.

Printed in Great Britain
by Amazon